# Some
# Assembly Required

### And Other Sermons for Advent

# Some Assembly Required

## And Other Sermons for Advent

Includes Accompanying Pastoral Prayers
and Children's Lessons

## Rev. Erskine White

## C.S.S. Publishing Co., Inc.

**Lima, Ohio**

# SOME ASSEMBLY REQUIRED

---

**Library of Congress Cataloging-in-Publication Data**

White, Erskine, 1951-
    Some assembly required, and other sermons for Advent / by Erskine
White.
      p.   cm.
    ISBN 1-55673-142-6
    1. Advent sermons.   2. Christmas sermons.   3. Sermons, American.
I. Title.
BV40.W47    1989
252'.61--dc20                                  89-10002
                                                           CIP

---

9867 / ISBN 1-55673-142-6

# Table of Contents

Dedicated
To my wife, Caroline,
and to our children:
Daniel, Joshua, and Jordan

*"We Are Family"*

# Foreword

"Study hard," the Reformed pastor Richard Baxter wrote, "for the well is deep, and our brains are shallow. But especially be laborious in practice and in the exercise of your knowledge." It is significant to me that the sermons and children's meditations offered in this little volume, came to life for the first time in the midst of the work of a deeply committed Christian congregation in an inner-city neighborhood. For the members of Friedens United Church of Christ, Milwaukee, the Gospel served as comfort, challenge, hope; a summons to discipleship both sincere and joyful. These sermons did not take shape alongside some luminous cloud in the sky, far-removed from the daily chores of the congregation. Instead, they came into being close to hard choices and deep searching for ways in which the church could remain faithful to its vocation. Friedens was not a place for "sloth, snoring, and sleeping" (Luther), for the congregation believed that when it comes to the significance of God's Word, the Gospel is at the very heart of all a Christian community shares, suffers, and hopes together.

I am pleased to commend these sermons and meditations to you as the work of a pastor who has sought, with all his human limitations and need, to combine prayerful study of the Scriptures with the practice and exercise of faith. He is among those who know that in the companionship of word and deed, the Gospel is most fully expressed and most responsibly addressed to the community of believers and to the world into which we are sent as ambassadors of Christ. May your spirit be refreshed as you reflect on the message contained in this book and may your faith be deepened as well that, as the old Advent hymn assures us: "Hark, the glad sound, the

Saviour comes, the Saviour promised long: Let every heart prepare a throne, And every voice a song . . . . And every voice a song.''

Frederick R. Trost
President
Wisconsin Conference of the
    United Church of Christ
Madison, Wisconsin

# Introduction

After preaching just a dozen sermons as a young pastor in his first church, the great theologian, Reinhold Niebuhr, worried that he had run out of ideas and was repeating himself.[1]

After preaching for a dozen (or more!) *years,* even the most indefatigable pastor can begin to feel the same way about Advent. After all, the Christmas story and its attendant texts don't change — how can one approach the Advent season year after year without running out of ideas or repeating oneself?

Similarly, the dedicated layperson looking for spirit and inspiration at Christmas time can also feel that "there is nothing new under the sun" insofar as the Advent season is concerned. How often can one put new wine in old wineskins? How often can one find new inspiration in a story which is so familiar?

Despite the difficulty, it is important to continue preaching and praying the special seasons of the Christian year, such as Advent. In spiritual terms, it is important to the individual believer and to the church as well. It is hoped that the sermons, prayers, and children's lessons in this little book will offer a few new Advent ideas to preachers or laypersons who are looking for them.

Readers will find a wide variety of styles within these pages. One sermon is didactic, another is pastoral, while still another is a story sermon. One sermon aims to be light-hearted and humorous, while another is seriously prophetic, and so on. Despite their diverse approaches, however, the heart of all these sermons is to proclaim the good news of Jesus Christ in faithfulness to the Scriptures.

Readers will further notice that a balance between pastoral and prophetic messages is maintained throughout the book

---

[1]Niebuhr kept an interesting and still-timely diary during his early years in the parish: *Leaves From the Notebook of a Tamed Cynic,* re-issued in 1980 by Harper and Row Publishers, Inc.

11

— the latter is not confined to a "Social Concerns Sunday" but is closely interwoven with the former throughout the weeks of Advent.

Finally, I hope another challenge has been met in these sermons: the challenge of maintaining the spirit of joy and anticipation which characterizes Advent without sacrificing the Christian message of the season. As many people have aptly noted, the minister's job is inherently difficult because he or she must preach gospel values which are fundamentally at odds with the dominant values of the surrounding culture. Year in and year out, and generation after generation, this remains the continuing challenge of Advent preaching and spirituality.

*Rev. Erskine White*
*Melrose, Massachusetts*

# A Word about Language

The language in this book pertaining to people is inclusive of men and women. Similarly, the anecdotes and illustrations have been deliberately varied so as to include the experiences of women and men alike. As for the language pertaining to God, it is necessary from time to time to use a pronoun for God, in order to preserve the biblical view that ours is a personal God. Whenever it appears, however, the pronoun is always preceded by a capital "H" to indicate to the reader that God is neither male nor female in human terms.

# The Secret Story of Gabriel

**Text:** Luke 1:26-38

*In the sixth month the angel Gabriel was sent from God to a city of Galilee named Nazareth . . . . (Luke 1:26)*

From our text in Luke you have heard the Bible's account of how God sent the angel Gabriel to Mary. But this is not the only version of the story. There is another, unofficial, version which came to light recently when an ancient manuscript was discovered in Bethlehem. For those of us who like to stay on the cutting edge of biblical research, this new discovery is exciting and has changed forever the way we know the story of Gabriel. It took the experts a long time to translate this manuscript because it was so badly faded and worn. In addition, some ancient homemaker had used part of it to make out a shopping list. But now, at long last, the Bethlehem manuscript is available in English. I am pleased to share with you the unofficial story — the secret story of Gabriel.

It seems that God had a problem. He had given His law and sent His prophets; but it wasn't enough. People were still lost in darkness and despair. Violence and corruption filled the earth while justice and mercy were on the run. God knew He had to do more than He had ever done before. He had to offer salvation by coming to the world Himself. But how would He do it? How would He announce it? How would He introduce His only begotten Son to the world? This was the problem God was trying to solve.

He needed some good advice, so He called the angel Gabriel into His office. We learn from this ancient manuscript that Gabriel wasn't just an angel with a trumpet. He was also in

15

charge of Peace and Goodwill Associates — God's public relations and advertising company. This is why God called Gabriel into His office; he seemed the perfect angel for the job.

Gabriel came in and before he could sit down, God started to speak. "Gabriel, I've decided to send My Son to save the world, but I can't decide on how He should be born. How can I best show by His birth what My Word looks like in the flesh? Put your best angels on it, Gabriel. This is the most important assignment your agency will ever get, so do a good job."

Gabriel went down to his office on Cloud Nine, gathered his brightest young angels around him, and they began to work. Finally, he was ready to go back and show his ideas to God.

He could hardly contain himself as he burst into God's office. "I've got it," he said. "I've got just the campaign You need, God! You'll love it, and You'll thank Your lucky stars that You gave this account to Peace and Goodwill Associates!

"You have to remember," Gabriel continued, "that this will be the most extraordinary event in the history of the world. God Himself is coming to earth! So what You need is the most awesome, most elaborate advertising campaign ever imagined. Money is no object. Your Child deserves nothing but the best."

Gabriel pulled out his flip charts and market research; he was ready to roll. "I thought we might start off low-key, and then go to an all-out media blitz. We start by printing millions of T-shirts and bumper stickers that simply say, 'He's coming!' Isn't it great! It's the oldest marketing trick in the book — you get people's attention and make them curious to learn more.

"Then we get someone to ghost-write a book for Joseph and Mary. It doesn't matter what's in the book — no one actually reads anymore. The important thing is that with a book to sell, we can get on the talk show circuit. Donahue or Winfrey might be good; they love stuff like this. A young virgin giving birth! They'll flip for it. It's right up their alley.

"We can't forget the Christian talk shows, God. They've got their own satellite networks now, and lots of people watch these shows. But first we'll have to change Joseph and Mary a bit. For one thing, they'll need some nicer clothes. You've got to look happy and successful to be on Christian television!

"And that Magnificat Mary wants to say — that bit about the hungry being filled with good things and the rich being sent away empty (Luke 1:53) — she's got to knock that off right away. The Christian talk shows won't stand for it! Prosperity sells, God; the audience wants comfort and blessings. If we're going to put Mary and Joseph on Christian television, they'll first need some coaching on what to say.

"But we need more than this, God. We need some prime time exposure. I suggest a Barbara Walters special. When you're interviewed by Barbara Walters, you *know* you've made it! And then we'll really hit the big time: we'll make the cover of *Time* and *Newsweek*. Maybe *Ms.* magazine would do a story on Mary. How much better could it get?"

By this point, Gabriel was really getting excited. Now he was ready for the climax — the big finish. "You have to realize," he said, "that *where* this Child is born is very important. We need to consider what kind of image we want the television cameras to show. I suggest we build the most magnificent palace the world has ever seen . . . a palace truly fit for the King of kings and Lord of lords. Remember: Your Child gets nothing but the best.

"And look, God, December 25th is a terrible day — a nothing day. Delay the birth a few weeks to mid-January, Super Bowl Sunday. Most people think it's the most important day of the year anyway. You'll have a huge captive audience; everyone will be sitting at home glued to their television sets.

"Then what You do, God, is to take over the airwaves during halftime, and broadcast the birth live. (But make sure You keep it to thirty minutes. You don't want to get people mad by delaying the rest of the game!) Have the world leaders bring gifts to the baby . . . they'll be glad to do it, especially if you promise them good TV coverage. Have the heavens open up and the angels sing. I tell you, God: this will be the greatest show ever!

"It will be better than the Olympics, even bigger than 'Who Shot J.R.?' Then after the birth, there will be a sound track album, music videos, a movie deal, Mary and Joseph dolls . . ."

God had heard enough. "No, no, no!" His voice thundered through the heavens. "You've got it all wrong! You've missed the point entirely! Do you think your gala can convey what this Child is all about? Does He need the blessing of TV preachers or *Newsweek* magazine? You haven't understood at all!

"And what do you think would happen if Jesus were born in a palace? Why, the whole thing would be turned into an inaugural ball, with black tie, evening gowns, and chauffeured limousines. They'd keep the common people locked outside the palace gate, far away from the face of Jesus.

"No one can claim this Child for himself, Gabriel. He is not sent just to mingle with the rich and famous. He is coming for all the people — even for the forgotten and despised, the sorrowful and lonely — even for the dust of the earth. He is coming for those who think they least deserve Him. He is born to show God's love, Gabriel. The glory of the Lord shall be revealed in this Child, and all flesh shall see it together!

"And what makes you think presidents and prime ministers would welcome this Child who comes to establish another kingdom not of this world and higher than their own? Don't you see that the shadow of the Cross will fall over Jesus even at the moment of His birth? People with power will pretend to praise Him while they plot to kill Him! No, Gabriel, if you want this Child to live, I wouldn't advertise too much when and where He is born. Least of all, don't tell the kings and queens where He is.

"Go back to your office and try again, Gabriel," God said. "You've been seduced by the celebrity culture and confused by the piety of popular preachers. Go back and read the prophets: *'For My thoughts are not your thoughts, neither are your ways My ways, says the Lord.' (Isaiah 55:8)* Come back tomorrow and if you don't have a better idea than this, I'll make sure that Peace and Goodwill Associates never works in heaven again!''

The ancient manuscript says that Gabriel came back the next day a chastened and contrite angel. He came back more concerned with mystery than marketing. He was ready to try again.

"You were right, God," he said. "I mimicked the world and missed Your Word. But now I've got a plan which is more faithful to Your ways. With my new plan people can reflect on how You chose to come into the world, and maybe then, they will come to understand You better than they do today."

"Go ahead, let's hear it," God said. "Every one deserves a second chance — even you."

"Well," said Gabriel, "I realize now that people would expect Christ to come as I expected Him to come: with all the fanfare and glory. In their pride, people would expect Christ to be welcomed with glad hearts and open arms in this fallen world. But we'll have Jesus come quietly, almost unnoticed, save for a few lowly shepherds and some travellers passing through.

"And forget the palace . . . it was a bad idea. People would expect a palace, but that's *their* expectation, not God's. We'll have Jesus born in a stable. He'll be homeless and laid in a humble manger on the edge of town. He'll be born in the kind of place respectable people hurry by on their way to some-place else.

"In this way," said Gabriel, "people might reflect on *how* He was born and get a better idea of what Your Word looks like in the flesh. Maybe this will help them love one another as God has loved each of them, and maybe this will show them the path to salvation."

At last God was pleased. "You have done well," He said. "You have captured My intention perfectly. This is how we will do it. We will take the world's vain expectations and turn them upside down. We will proclaim, even by the manner of His birth, that in God's Kingdom the first are last and the last are first.''

That is the secret story of Gabriel. The ancient manuscript concludes by saying that Gabriel went on to have a long and successful career with Peace and Goodwill Associates. He landed many other heavenly advertising accounts and eventually moved his office to the penthouse suite on Cloud Ninty-Nine.

Fortunately, this unofficial story will never find its way into Scripture, but there is a message here nonetheless: you won't find the Christ Child in the familiar places where the world in its vanity would expect Him to be. You won't find Him on television extravaganzas with the celebrities of church or state or business — you won't find Him in Crystal Cathedrals on Christmas Eve. Nor will you find Him in the gaudy displays or bright lights of the holiday season. No, you must find Him in the quietness of your hearts, in the peace and humility of one who looks for God's glory in a lowly manger. "How silently, how silently, the wondrous gift is given!" God chooses to come to us! We need eyes to see and ears to hear, for lo, our salvation is drawing near. Amen

# Pastoral Prayer

Faithful and Merciful God, who is our Comfort and Strength from age to age, we pray today for all who are weary of body or spirit. We pray for those who suffer pain, and the infirmities of age. We pray for the sick and the lonely, and for those with restless spirits and unsatisfied minds. Help everyone in need to find their rest in You, O God. Bring comfort to those who hurt, and strength to those who mourn. Be as real to us as the ground beneath our feet, O Lord, and help us plainly every step along the way.

Almighty, Everlasting God, who has taken the form of a helpless baby lying homeless in a bed of straw, lead us to find You in the quiet places of simple faith this Christmas season. Lead us in the paths of lowliness and meekness, that there we may find our Lord. Open our eyes and ears to the silent, holy night; help us to see the baby and hear His cry, and know that He is born. In Jesus' name we pray. Amen

# Who Are Your Angels?

*In the sixth month the angel Gabriel was sent from God to a city of Galilee named Nazareth . . . . (Luke 1:26)*

What do you think angels look like? *(Let them answer.)*

*Have you ever seen an angel? (Let them answer again).* Be careful now: you may have seen pictures or cartoons of angels, but do you think you've ever met a real, live angel?

The Bible says that not many of us ever get to see an angel. After all, there are thousands of people in the pages of the Bible, and only a very few of them actually see angels face-to-face. Mary was one of the lucky few — she saw the angel Gabriel, whom God had sent to Nazareth to tell Mary that she would be the mother of God's Son, Jesus.

We don't have to see angels to believe they are real. God "made all things that are in heaven and earth, visible and invisible." (Colossians 1:16) You can't see the breath coming out of your mouths, but you know you are breathing! You can't see things like love or happiness, but you know they are real. There's a lot more to God's world than just what meets the eye, so we can believe in angels even if we can't see them.

When God sent His angel to visit Mary, He made her the happiest mother in the world. But angels aren't just for a few people in the Bible like Mary. God sends angels to us, too! That's right: God sends angels — another kind of angel — to help us, to look after us, to give us guidance and direction in life. These angels who are visible to us may not have wings or fly around in the air like Gabriel, but God still sends "angels" to us just the same. Do you know who *your* angels are . . . the people who are helping you in life?

What about your parents? Don't they love you and care for you . . . won't they stand by you no matter what? God gave you parents just for that reason, to guide and protect you while you are growing up in this world. We all need someone to turn to; I hope each of you can feel that your parents are your first "angels" in life.

What about other "angels"? Do you have a teacher who really helps you and cares about you, a Sunday school teacher or a weekday teacher? What about your minister? A family friend? What about your grandparents, aunts, or uncles? I'll bet if you think about it, you could name several "angels" in your life . . . people you can always count on to care about you when you need it the most.

Sometimes growing up is confusing and even scary, so it's good to know that you are not alone. Young and old, we all have people we can turn to who make a real difference in our lives — they are like angels sent by God to help us. Who are *your* angels? Amen

# The Rest of the Christmas Story

**Old Testament Text:** Isaiah 40:1-5
**New Testament Text:** Luke 1:39-42, 46-56

*He has scattered the proud in the imagination of their hearts . . .*
*and exalted those of low degree. (Luke 1:51-52)*

You might say there are three aspects of the Christmas season, three levels to the meaning of Christmas. Most Americans are familiar with the first two and largely unaware of the third.

We are all familiar with the first aspect of Christmas, the commercialism. It is everywhere around us, an unrelenting cacophony of hype and hoopla which begins before the Thanksgiving dishes are done and doesn't end until Christmas Eve.

"What am I going to get? What did so-and-so get us last year . . . We don't want to give them too much or too little this year."

At this first level Christmas is for buying things, or more particular, for buying now and paying later. Christmas is about business. The big question is whether we will spend enough money and take on enough debt to make it a good season for the merchants. "Will it be a good Christmas year?" Wall Street and chambers of commerce and credit card companies all want to know.

Most of all, Christmas is noisy. The cry of mammon's babble never stops. In fact, it gets louder each year as the "talk-fast-and-scream" school of advertising takes over the airwaves. Christmas reduced to sales and Santa is joyless and exhausting. The spirit is crushed under the dead weight of worldliness.

25

Many people, even many Christians, just drift along with the noise and frenzy. They figure it's all a part of living in the "good old U.S. of A," in the culture of the Almighty Dollar. But other Christians are not satisfied with that. They don't surrender to the noise or capitulate to the commercialism. They reach for a second level, a higher level, where the meaning of Christmas is more spiritual and centered on Christ.

These Christians make spiritual space in their homes and hearts for the birth of our Lord. They read the Bible and share Advent devotions. They talk to children not about Santa Claus, but about Jesus Christ. In short, those who seek a better way at Christmas do everything they can to resist what Scripture calls the "love of this present world" (cf 2 Timothy 4:10), because

*Where meek souls will receive Him still,*
*The dear Christ enters in.*

It takes a conscious effort to reach this higher spiritual level of Christmas. It is a struggle to overcome the love of money in the world. But amid all of the noise, we can still come to the quiet stable. Even as advertisers scream about Christmas sales, we can hear the angels sing. We can see the star's light shining bright. For those who seek it, Christmas is still a quiet miracle wrought by God on a silent and holy night.

The birth of Jesus, of course, is the second familiar aspect of Christmas. It is a season for faith and spiritual renewal . . . a time for family reunions and holiday parties . . . a time for "chestnuts roasting on an open fire."

But even this is just a part of the Christmas spirit. You can rise above the commercialism to that higher spiritual level where Christmas is the joy of Christ in your heart and home. You can do that and celebrate the season in spirit with family and friends, yet still not know the rest of the Christmas story.

The rest of the story is social. It is a radical vision, a revolutionary hope, a promise made through Jesus Christ of things begun and things to come. This is the part most of us are least familiar with, but the birth of Jesus Christ is also the birth of the kingdom of God in its early glory for all the world to see. Scripture tells us this almost on every page, wherever prophets speak and angels sing about the meaning of Christmas.

Isaiah first said it 700 years before Christ was born. Here in our text for this morning, he says, "Prepare the way of the Lord!" He says that with the coming of our Savior — our Prince of Peace — everything will change, even the land itself:

*Every valley shall be lifted up,*
*and every mountain and hill be made low;*
*the uneven ground shall become level,*
*and the rough places smooth.*
*And the glory of the Lord shall be revealed,*
*and all flesh shall see it together.*     *(Isaiah 40:4-5)*

Now we come to our New Testament text from Luke and see what Mary says about the meaning of Christ's birth:

*[The Lord] has scattered the proud in the*
    *imagination of their hearts;*
*He has put down the mighty from their thrones,*
*and exalted those of low degree;*
*He has filled the hungry with good things,*
*and the rich He has sent empty away.*     *(Luke 1:51-53)*

Even when Jesus is born, the angels sing about Christmas in its larger, social context:

*Glory to God in the highest, and on earth peace*
*among [all people], with whom He is pleased!(Luke 2:14)*

And finally, when Jesus is grown and begins His ministry, He goes back to quote Isaiah, and these are the very first words He says:

> *The Spirit of the Lord is upon Me,*
> *because He has annointed Me to preach*
> *good news to the poor.*
> *He has sent Me to proclaim release*
> *to the captives . . . [and] to set*
> *at liberty those who are oppressed . . .*    *(Luke 4:18)*

There it is: a consistent message from beginning to end on the larger meaning of Christmas. It is spoken by prophets and angels and Mary — and by Jesus Himself. Christmas in its fullness is social: a vision of justice and peace — a promise of *shalom*.

The Bible does not reduce Christ, as many Christians do, to merely a "personal" Savior. The Bible says He comes to save the world! The whole world is changed by His birth! Our whole moral geography is uprooted and rearranged as valleys are lifted up and mountains made low. Good news is preached to the poor, and the rich are sent empty away. So, Merry Christmas to one and all! By God's Word, this is the rest of the Christmas story.

I dare say that millions of people around the world are eager to hear this story today. From Harlem to Hong Kong, faithful people everywhere want to know that God has *"scattered the proud in the imagination of their hearts, [and] put down the mighty from their thrones, and exalted those of low degree." (Luke 1:51-52)* When we love God's Word and want the valleys lifted up today, we know that Christmas is more than petty commercialism, and more than a narrow faith in a personal Savior.

To fully appreciate this larger meaning of the Christmas season, perhaps we can use our moral imaginations today. Let us imagine that we are someone else — someone in the world who might desperately want to hear the rest of the Christmas story.

Imagine you are a black South African in this Christmas season. You are thirty-five years old, with a wife and two children. What does the coming of Christmas mean to you?

Because you are black, your family has been assigned to live in a "black area" (a *bantustan),* akin to a reservation. It is land the white people don't want, poor land with poor jobs. The better jobs are in the "white areas," so you have gone there to work. You feel you are lucky to have your job, but you earn a quarter of a white man's wage for your labor. Because you are black, your family cannot follow you to your job. You may remain temporarily in a white area because you have a useful skill: but your wife and children have no useful skills, so they must stay on the "reservation." You live in a barracks next to your factory with fifty other men who, like yourself, are forced by apartheid to leave their families to be able to provide for them.

Because you are black, you must send your children to grievously inferior schools; the state spends eight times as much money educating a white child as it spends on your child. Meanwhile, the official curriculum teaches your children that they are inferior because of their race. In turn, the official state religion uses the Bible to say that the whites of South Africa are God's chosen people.

Because you are black, you pray that your children don't get sick. There is one doctor for every 91,000 blacks, compared to one doctor for every 330 whites.

You may join a union, but if you go on strike, you can be sent to jail. If you join a rent strike, or any other form of nonviolent protest against apartheid, you can be sent to jail. If you urge that American corporations divest and leave your country, you can be sent to jail. If you shelter someone who is in a white area looking for work, you can be sent to jail. And if you do disappear into jail, you can only hope they don't torture you.

Because you are black, you, or your wife, or even your children, can be arrested at any time by any agent of the state for any reason whatsoever — or for no reason at all. That's the law in the "state of emergency." They can burst into your home whenever they choose. They can literally shoot you on sight, in the street or in your bed, and do it with impunity.

In short, as a black South African, you live under the most repressive regime on earth — more repressive even than Cuba or the Soviet Union. You live in fear of an overwhelming police force. You live in constant fear of government surveillance by paid informers and spies. And thanks to the "state of emergency," you live under the most rigorous press censorship in the world. You have no right to vote in a national election. You have no right to privacy and no right to peaceful protest. You don't even have the right to life, because you are black.

Everything I have just told you is true. This is how a great many black South Africans live today.

Now imagine that Christmas is here, and you can't go home. You gather with the men in your barracks to celebrate. You'll sing that Christ is born in Bethlehem; "Hark the herald angels sing, glory to the newborn King!" And you'll be glad for the birth of Jesus. You'll open your heart to Him and rededicate your life to Him, and seek Him out in the manger as the Wise Men did of old.

But more than that, I suspect that as a black South African, you'll want to hear the larger message of Christmas, too. You'll want to hear about valleys being lifted up, and rough places made smooth. Your soul will yearn to hear Isaiah say: *"Speak tenderly to Jerusalem, and cry to her that her warfare is ended." (Isaiah 40:2)*

You'll also want to hear Mary: *"He has shown strength with His arm, and scattered the proud in the imagination of their hearts . . . He has filled the hungry with good things, and the rich He has sent empty away." (Luke 1:51, 53)*

My friends, the larger meaning of Christmas is social, and you have been hearing it. For people of faith everywhere who hunger and thirst for what is right, Christ is born to "put down the mighty from their thrones, and exalt those of low degree."

This is also why He comes . . . Hope of the world. And now, we are more ready to receive Him in this Advent season. Now, we are ready to know more perfectly the love of God in Christ Jesus, because now we know the rest of the Christmas story. Amen

# Pastoral Prayer

Almighty and Everlasting Lord, who comes to us this Advent season as Mary's baby, wrapped in swaddling clothes and laid in a bed of straw: help us to find that humble place, that where He is, there we may be also. Help us to open our hearts to Him as the blessed day approaches. Free our minds from all worldly distractions which might keep us away from the manger. Make this Christmas truly the time when we come to see Him in spirit and in truth.

Most Holy, Most Righteous God, to whom the nations are accounted as dust on the scales of time, we also pray that we may hear the rest of the Christmas story today. Help all of us to see how this lowly baby throws down what is mighty and exalts what is humble. Make us eager for the day when every valley is lifted up and every rough place is made smooth, and every injustice is swept away before the coming of the Lord. Help us to worship today with people everywhere who hunger and thirst for what is right, that Your will may yet be done on earth, even as it is done in heaven. In Jesus' name we pray. Amen

# God's Special Mission for You

*". . . for [God] has regarded the low estate of His handmaiden."*
*(Luke 1:48)*

You've all heard us speak of Mary in church this Christmas season: do you know what is really so amazing about Mary? *(Let them answer)* It's not just that she was the mother of Jesus, which is pretty amazing in itself. No, I think the most amazing thing about Mary is that she was such an ordinary person.

Mary was just a young teenager when God chose her to be Jesus' mother; in fact, she wasn't much older than some of you. She lived in a small town in a small house with her parents and the rest of her family. Everything about her life was ordinary.

The Bible doesn't give any particular reason to explain why Mary was chosen by God. It doesn't say she was especially smart or unusually pretty. It doesn't say she was the best-known or most popular girl in town. We know she wasn't from a rich or important family; in fact, Mary came from a rather poor and simple family. In other words, Mary was just an average, everyday child . . . the kind you play with or go to school with . . . a lot like any of us . . . a lot like any one of you.

Sometimes, we get the wrong idea about the Bible stories we learn in Sunday school. We learn about people like Moses, Samson, Ruth, or Deborah. We hear exciting stories like Daniel in the lion's den or David and Goliath and we think that everyone who does something special for God must be exceptionally strong or brave or bright, and then we think that God couldn't possibly have any use for us since we are all quite ordinary people.

Well, the truth is that most of the people in the Bible are not superheroes; most of them are average people like us, with their own strengths and weaknesses. But, it's also true that God had a special mission for every one of them just the same.

God's special mission for Mary was to give birth to His only Son, Jesus. He picked an ordinary girl for the job, but Mary had one quality that was very important. She had a spirit which said "yes" when God asked her to do something.

What do you think God's special mission is for you? If you imagine that you are God's secret agent, what might your assignment be?

Right now, your mission might be to love your family, to learn and grow; surely God has that in mind for all of you. But what about when you are older; what special mission might God have for you then? If you are the kind of person who will say "yes" to God, He will have you to do something very important for Him in this world. God has a special mission for everyone, including you. Won't it be fun, as you grow older and get to know God better to find out what God's special mission for you might be? Amen

# The Changes Children Bring

**Text:** Isaiah 11:1-9

*. . . and a little child shall lead them. (Isaiah 11:6)*

During the last five years my wife and I have found out what every other parent in all of human history has found out: children bring changes to your life. In fact, children take life as you've known it and turn it upside down.

In his book, *Fatherhood,* Bill Cosby asks just one question of those who want to have children: Why? "Why would you have children when all your other acts were rational?" Why would you give up the comfortable patterns of your life for "the joys of frantically coping with reproductions of yourselves?"

Think of all the changes children bring.

Once, it didn't matter where you kept things in the house. You could put products like cleaning liquid or razor blades wherever it was most convenient to use them.

But when the children come — forget it! You are now engaged in a kind of guerilla warfare against diabolically clever creatures who are equipped with a built-in radar system to help them find all the things they shouldn't find.

If the box of cereal is stored on the bottom shelf in the kitchen, the whole floor will be covered with Cheerios or Froot Loops. If your delicate drinking glasses are left on the counter, your children will prove that glass breaks when it is thrown to the floor with sufficient force. The cleaning liquid must be stored high above reach, or it will end up in someone's mouth.

In other words, children bring radical changes to your house or apartment. You have to rearrange everything and "childproof" every room until the children are old enough to "know better."

Once, you could put something down in a certain place, and it would still be there when you went back for it. But when the children come — forget it! For example, I have had a certain hair brush for years. In fact, it was given to me when I was eight by a friend of the family, and ever since then, I have used that same hairbrush and kept it in the same place on my dresser. Until I had children, that is. The other day as I was getting ready for work, I couldn't find my hairbrush. In fact, I couldn't find it for three days. It stayed lost until I went to make a snack one night, and there was my hairbrush, sitting in the toaster oven! That's another change children bring — nothing stays where you left it unless it is nailed down.

Once, you had such a thing as peace and quiet. You could get all your work done and joyously make plans to sit down and watch your favorite team in the most important game of the year. But when the children come — forget it! Just as the game is set to begin, the baby wakes up from a nap and the other children both want to play with the same toy. A huge Tonka truck comes hurtling down the stairs and you have to go find out why. You remember Jesus' words, *"Blessed are the peacemakers, for they shall be called children of God,"* *(Matthew 5:9)* but by the time you get back to the game, it's half over.

Yes, children bring changes. They "turn couches into trampolines." (Cosby, *Fatherhood*) They turn your king-sized bed into a giant toy box. When you climb into bed at night and impale yourself on the sharp point of a plastic toy which somehow found its way under your sheets, you say to yourself, "I remember when this bed was just a bed. I remember when hairbrushes didn't end up in toaster ovens. I remember when . . ."

Yes, children bring changes. They take silent homes and fill them with laughter and the sound of running feet. They take lives which never knew how empty they were and fill them with love and joy and the sparkling light of dancing eyes. Children bring blessing upon blessing to their parents, and even though they change our lives in hundreds of ways both great and small, we love them dearly and wouldn't have it any other way.

Can we say the same thing about the Christ Child, who is soon to be born in our midst? If our own children change our lives in so many earthly ways, shouldn't the baby Jesus change our lives even more profoundly, and for all eternity?

Two women were standing on the corner of a busy downtown street at the height of the Christmas season. The cars were bumper to bumper, so the women could barely cross the street. They stood there on the sidewalk with presents piled high over their heads, but the sidewalks were as crowded as the street with people pushing and rushing to get their shopping done. Sometimes the people were friendly; sometimes they were rude as they tried to get their gifts before anyone else did.

"I hate Christmas," one woman said to the other. "I hate all the crowds and the noise, the rat race of commercialism, the confusion, the short tempers people have, and the expensive things you're expected to buy. To me, Christmas is frustrating."

"Well, I'm sorry you feel that way," the other woman said, "because I love Christmas. To think that a little Child born 2,000 years ago halfway around the world could create such an uproar in the middle of this modern city — it's just amazing!"

It's true, isn't it, that this one Child born in Bethlehem puts the world into an uproar every year at this time? This one Child creates enormous changes throughout the world: at least in an outward, superficial sense with the lights and sales and loudspeakers with Christmas music wafting over busy streets. But what about the inner changes, the deeper changes this Christ Child can bring to your life?

The prophet Isaiah spoke of all that would happen when the Messiah comes, and he said, *"A little child shall lead them."* One little Child! His name is Jesus, and when He is born, nothing is ever the same again.

What about you? Once this baby is born, will your life be any different because of Him? Will you put aside your old ways to take on the cost and joy of discipleship in His name? We all know that children bring changes in life. What changes will this Child bring to your life on Christmas Day? Amen

# Pastoral Prayer

Most Blessed God, who sent a little Child to lead us from darkness to light, make us open to the changes this Child will bring to our lives. Make us ready to be more loving and more giving. Make us ready to find ourselves by losing ourselves in Him. Most of all, dear God, help us to follow Him on a journey to salvation. Help us, through this Child, to give up the lives we have known for a greater life in Him. Through Jesus Christ we pray. Amen

# Your Family Tree

*"There shall come forth a shoot from the stump of Jesse . . ." (Isaiah 11:1)*

*[Note: For this lesson, you may want to cut a piece of construction paper into the shape of a tree, and give each child a "branch" to take home. If your church has a Christmas tree in the sanctuary during Advent, you might distribute small pieces from the branches of the tree.]*

I'm giving you these branches because I want you to remember to do something this Christmas season. If you will be seeing your grandparents or older relatives for the holidays, I want you to ask them to tell you something about your family tree. I don't mean the kind of tree that grows in the yard near your home. A family tree is something that tells you where you came from. It tells you about your ancestors . . . the people in your family who lived many years before you were born, your great-grandparents, and their grandparents, and their grandparents before them.

It might be fun to see some old family pictures, to look at the clothes they wore and try to imagine what it was like to live in "the old days." What do you think children did before they had MTV or radio or movies or cartoons to fill their time? What do you think life was like before electric lights or cars or ten-speed bikes? Ask your grandparents, and they'll be able to tell you what they know or what they heard when they were young like you.

Sometimes you can find some interesting stories in your family tree. Maybe one of your ancestors was a cowboy or a pioneer woman in the Old West. Maybe your ancestors came from Europe or Asia or the Caribbean or Latin America; maybe they were brought here from Africa. In any case, you can probably better understand who you are today by learning something about where your family came from.

Jesus had a family tree, too. In fact, one of Jesus' ancestors was very famous: he was the best-loved king of Israel, King David. When he was a young boy, David fought a giant named Goliath and killed him with a slingshot. He did many other brave and heroic things when he became a man. I imagine that when Jesus was growing up, He heard lots of stories about His famous ancestor, the great King David.

But Jesus doesn't belong to just one family, the family of David. Jesus is God's Son and when Jesus was born, He started a whole new family tree, one which includes all of us. That's right! We are all descended from Jesus; in a Christian sense, we are all part of the same family tree.

Jesus said that He is the vine from which all our branches grow. (John 15:5) He said He came to this world to make all people one. (John 17:21) Jesus said that anyone who does God's will is His brother and sister. (Matthew 12:50) That's what I mean when I say that we are all part of one family tree.

If you look closely at the branches I've given you this morning, you'll notice that they are all different from one another. No two branches are exactly alike because each of our families is different. Each family has a unique story to tell.

But notice also that all of these branches come from the same tree, the same root. That tree and that root is Jesus. He made us all part of the same family because He wants us to love each other as brothers and sisters, to live together as children of God. So, maybe you could ask someone at home to help you draw a family tree. But before you are done, remember to put at the root of your family tree the most important name of all . . . the name of Jesus. Amen

## A Most Amazing Night

**Text:** Luke 2:1-20

*"But Mary kept all these things, pondering them in her heart. (Luke 2:19)*

The shadows are getting long in late afternoon as Joseph comes running into the house bursting with news: Caesar Augustus has ordered a census for the whole Roman Empire. Everyone will have to go to their family's hometown to be counted and to pay a tax. For Joseph and Mary, this means travelling to Bethlehem. Mary wants to know more, but Joseph can't answer her questions. The Romans are not in the habit of explaining themselves to simple carpenters from Nazareth. They just give the orders and expect them to be obeyed.

Mary cannot be happy about the news. She has had to bear one burden after another for months on end, ever since God chose her to carry a child conceived by His Holy Spirit. And now this decree comes down from Caesar. She and Joseph must get ready to travel, just when she is ready to deliver her first baby.

Mary is just a child herself, a girl of perhaps thirteen or fourteen. She and Joseph are betrothed, which is more than an engagement but less than a marriage. According to the law of the time, couples are betrothed for a year before getting married.

In short, Mary is a pregnant teenager — an unwed mother, if you will. It is not unknown in the ancient world to cast girls like her out of the village or even put them to death. Mary lives with such fears for nine months, and she faces the ridicule and shame of her friends and neighbors.

But Mary is blessed to have such a good man in Joseph. Incredibly, he believes her story! He accepts her fantastic insistence that she is still a virgin for him, and that this child comes by the Holy Spirit. He doesn't have to do it — and at first he struggles to take Mary at her word — but in the end, Joseph decides to stick with her and go through with the wedding.

Mary spends a few days packing and getting ready for the trip. She bakes some bread and dries some meat to eat along the way. She pours well water into the goatskin bags they will tie to the back of their donkey. Finally, she packs some blankets and swaddling clothes, strips of cloth to wrap around a newborn baby.

The journey to Bethlehem is a long, slow walk of ninety miles, up and down the rugged hillside. Mary rides the donkey and Joseph walks beside her, making sure the animal does not stumble. They stop when Mary needs to rest. With her swollen womb nearly ready to deliver, Mary feels every bounce, every rock or rut in the donkey's path, as they go to keep their date with Caesar.

The trip takes many days. The daytime sun is warm, but the nights are cold. As darkness falls, they look for a cave to sleep in, or at least a tree to shelter them by the side of the road. As they get closer to Bethlehem, the road is more crowded with other people making the same journey for the same reason. Now they must worry about thieves and pickpockets and other dangerous characters who make their livings in crowds like this.

Maybe, as they walk along the road, Joseph and Mary reflect on the inconvenience of it all. Today, food pantries across the land are overrun when a bill is signed in Washington, or whole communities die when a piece of paper is signed in some corporate board room. Well, so too as Joseph and Mary walk into Bethlehem: all of Israel is turned upside down when a man named Caesar signs a piece of paper in Rome.

There are Roman soldiers standing by, watching the people stream into town. They joke and laugh among themselves as the parade of nameless, faceless humanity passes before them. The soldiers are smug, secure in the knowledge that the power of Rome rules the world, now and forever.

Surely they don't notice Joseph and Mary in the crowd — a carpenter and a pregnant girl. Surely they never suspect that a child will be born here tonight who will eclipse the power of Caesar, and change the world in a way no Caesar ever could.

It is already late when Joseph and Mary begin looking for a room. They are turned away every time. "I have no vacancies," the innkeepers tell them, "and even if I had one, I couldn't rent it to you. Nothing personal, mind you; it's just that Caesar's order has really driven up the rents around here. This town is full of travellers tonight, so I must charge top dollar. I'm sorry the girl is pregnant, but business is business, you know."

Finally,they hear about a small cave on the edge of town, where poor and migrant people often stay. In front of the cave is a lean-to stable. Inside, there is some straw and a manger. Time is running out, so Joseph gets busy. He pushes the animals into the cave and makes a bed with his blanket in the straw. He builds a small fire to chase off the night chill. He pours some water out of the goatskin and asks his betrothed if there is anything else he can do to make her more comfortable.

Now the labor begins. Every woman who has born a child can imagine what young Mary goes through. But you have to imagine giving birth without painkillers or fetal monitors or any of the other conveniences we enjoy today. Mary is on her own.

She looks up and sees the dark, dank ceiling of the cave. To her right, she sees the animals, their breath from their nostrils becoming visible in the frigid air. She turns to her left and looks into the anxious eyes of her husband-to-be.

The pain of her labor wears on into the night. Then comes the final, excruciating moment of birth. Words from the book of Genesis flash through Mary's mind: *"In pain you shall bring forth children." (3:16b)* Finally, she hears the baby's cry and she slumps back onto the straw, too exhausted to move or even look at the child.

Mary only rests for an instant. Quickly, she recovers her senses and wraps the baby in the swaddling clothes she had packed in Nazareth. She holds Him close to protect Him from the cold, and puts Him to her breast to give Him His first meal.

Then, when the baby goes to sleep, she lays Him in a manger. There He is asleep on a bed of straw, lying in a manger in a donkey's stable! Thus is born into the world the King of kings and Lord of lords.

That same night there are shepherds in the fields, keeping watch over their flocks. For them, it is a night like any other; they are huddling by a warm fire, swapping stories and gossip. Some are dozing off. The rest keep watch and wait for the dawn.

Suddenly, there is a light around them which quickly grows until it is nearly bright as day. It shines as bright as the glory of the Lord. This light comes upon the midnight clear, with angels bending near the earth to touch their harps of gold.

The shepherds fall to the ground in fear, feebly trying to protect themselves when there is no protection to be found. Then they hear a voice:

> *Fear not, for behold, I bring you good news of a great joy which shall come to all people. For unto you is born this day in the city of David a Savior, who is Christ the Lord. And this shall be a sign for you: you shall find the babe wrapped in swaddling clothes and lying in a manger. (Luke 2:10-12)*

Now the shepherds are wide awake and filled with excitement. They rush to Bethlehem and search the stables until they find the baby Jesus. They gather around Him and marvel at the mysteries which are unfolding on this silent, holy night:

*Son of God, love's pure light*
*Radiant beams from His holy face,*
*With the dawn of redeeming grace,*
*Christ the Savior is born!*

The shepherds wave their calloused hands in the air as they tell Joseph and Mary about the great light. Their rough, weather-beaten faces appear to flicker in the firelight as they carefully repeat every word the angel said. Then they return to their flocks, rejoicing and praising God to everyone who will listen.

Emmanuel means "God with us." It began as a secret shared only by Mary and Elizabeth, the mother of John the Baptizer. Now it is starting to be known in all the world.

There are also three Wise Men from the east making their way to Bethlehem that night. They are Magi, or magicians . . . astrologers or scientists of their day. They are coming because they have seen a bright new star shining over Israel and they think something special is about to happen there.

They, too, find the baby. Even though He doesn't look very majestic lying there in a crude manger, the Wise Men worship Him and offer their gifts. They give gold, a symbol of kingship and worldly riches. They give frankincense, a fragrance symbolizing inner riches and spirituality. And they give myrrh, which is also considered precious in the ancient world. But then again, maybe the gift of myrrh has a double meaning since myrrh is also used in the ancient world to embalm the bodies of the dead.

Maybe the Wise Men warn Joseph and Mary that King Herod is already plotting to kill this baby. Maybe they speak earnestly about the danger this child poses to the world and the danger He faces from the world. Maybe even the beams from the stable form the shadow of a cross over the infant Jesus! Mary sees the Wise Men look at her deeply, and then they leave. Are they offering her their blessings or their sympathy?

We have no pictures of Mary, so we don't know what she looked like. But she has become a universal woman these last 2,000 years. European artists have made her look European. African artists have made her look African. In Japan, she is Japanese. Yet, every artist has made her look thoughtful and serene. What we *do* know about Mary is that she kept all the things she saw that night and pondered them in her heart. What a magnificent description of Mary — what a remarkable and insightful phrase! She "pondered them in her heart." It invites us to wonder what Mary thought about after the last Wise Man was gone. What would you have thought about?

Maybe she asked herself: "Why me? Why did God choose a poor, ordinary girl like me? He could have given this child a much easier start in life with some other mother! What did I do for God to single me out among all women?"

Maybe she wondered what this child would mean in her life. Already, she could see that He wasn't just given to her, but to the whole world. And she could already see that just by His birth, this tiny baby was a threat to the high and mighty of the earth: Herod wanted to kill Him! Perhaps Mary asked herself: "Why do they persecute the innocents for doing God's will? Why is the world so hostile to God's goodness and light?"

Does she anticipate the heartache this son will give her? Does she imagine that one day, Jesus will turn to her in front of a whole crowd of people and say, "I have no mother?" Does she suspect that the crowds will adore Him and then turn on Him in a fury? Does she foresee the day when she will stand beneath a cross and watch Him die?

Maybe Mary recalled the long, hard journey to Bethlehem, the search for a room to rent, and the agony of giving birth. Maybe she smiled wryly at the strange purposes of God, that He confounds the world by coming in the glory of a lowly manger. Maybe she remembered with a warm glow the simple shepherds, the sophisticated Wise Men, and the talk of stars and angels. Whatever she thought about as she lay there in the straw, Mary treasured this most amazing night, when all the world was changed. It was sacred, mysterious, and wonderful to behold:

*O holy night, the stars are brightly shining,*
*It is the night of the dear Savior's birth.*
*Long lay the world in sin and darkness pining,*
*Till He appeared, and the soul felt its worth.*

Jesus Christ comes to give every soul its worth. He takes upon Himself the sins of the world and brings God's light into our darkness. He comes that all people may find their peace in Him. He comes with the promise of everlasting life.

Never again can anyone say, "My salvation is too far away; I cannot reach it" — because now our salvation is very near.

On that most amazing night so long ago, good news of a great joy was given to all people, and we are heirs to that joy today. By faith, we are witnesses as God's only begotten Son is born into the world. Be like the shepherds, who came to see Him and rejoice. Be like the Wise Men, who came with their gifts of time and substance. But be like Mary, too, who kept the meaning of it all and pondered it in her heart. Amen

# Pastoral Prayer

Heavenly God, who sends angels with good news of great joy for all people, we pray that we will be bearers of good news in our time, according to Your Word. Give us grace to be a comfort for others. Grant to us a helpful word and a healing touch in the face of suffering. Help us show your light in all darkness and Your hope in all despair, that together we may be lifted up on the wings of Your promises, given in Christ Jesus, our Lord.

Everlasting Lord, fill us today with the real spirit of Christmas. Fill us with the awe of the shepherds, the wonder of the Wise Men, and the wisdom of Mary, who kept all things, pondering them in her heart. Lift our vision beyond the presents we get and the chores we do at Christmas time, and let us see the star to follow, that we may find the manger and look into the face of our salvation. Lead us to make that journey together, that we may lose ourselves in Him and live in purity and truth, from this day forward, and even for evermore. In Jesus' name we pray. Amen

**Children's Lesson**

# What the Angels Said

*"Glory to God in the highest and on earth peace among [all people] with whom He is pleased!" (Luke 2:14)*

Does anyone know who Caesar Augustus was? *(Let them answer)* That's right: he was the Emperor of Rome. Caesar Augustus was the most powerful man in the world. He had the world's biggest army. He conquered people everywhere and made them subjects of his empire. He was bigger and "badder" than Darth Vader! Why, the people around Caesar even said he was a god.

Caesar Augustus was so powerful that he could make the whole world move! It happened when he ordered everyone to return to their family's hometown, to be counted and pay a tax. Millions of people in many nations had to pick up their families and take a dangerous journey just because a man named Caesar told them to. That's why Joseph and Mary left Nazareth when Mary was ready to give birth, and why Jesus was born in Bethlehem.

If you had lived in those days, you would have heard your parents complaining about all this. There was great injustice in the world, which means that many people were treated unfairly. There was no freedom, because Caesar ruled with an iron hand. There was terrible poverty and life was hard. Most families and most children had to scratch their way just to survive.

The sad thing is that little has changed since then. Life is still hard for most families and most children in the world today. Millions of people still have to scratch their ways just to survive — here in America and around the world. The

51

rich still enjoy themselves while the poor still suffer, just as it was in Bible times. *(e.g. Jeremiah 4:26-31; Amos 4:1-3)*

Millions of children today have mothers or fathers who work, but they don't get paid enough to take care of their families. Millions of children today have no home at all . . . they must beg for food by day and sleep in the streets at night. Christmas is coming for them, too, just as it is coming for you and me.

That's why, on the night Jesus was born, the angels gave a special message to the world: *"Glory to God in the highest, and on earth peace among [all people] with whom He is pleased!"* You see, the angels remind us that there is more to Christmas than gifts or family get-togethers. The birth of Jesus at Christmas is also God's promise that someday there will be a better world. Someday no child anywhere will be homeless or hungry. The Caesars will be gone, and peace will cover all the earth. For your sake, and for the sake of children everywhere, let's hope that day comes soon. Merry Christmas to one and all! Amen

# What Are You Giving This Year?

What are you giving for Christmas this year? Oh, I know the usual question is, "What are you getting for Christmas?" but tonight I'm asking, "What are you *giving* for Christmas this year?"

As we get older we learn that giving is more fun than receiving during the holiday season. I mean — after so many years of getting presents, what is left? What is new? You may be glad to get a new sweater or a new shirt for Christmas, but you've got other clothes in the closet. In my case, I'm happy to get Bruce Springsteen's latest album, but I've got other record albums.

No, it's the giving that makes Christmas fun. It's seeing the shock on someone's face when you really surprise her, or seeing the joy when you give her something she dearly wanted. It's also the humor of silly gifts: my poor grandfather used to get a hair brush or a bottle of shampoo every year for Christmas, and he was as bald as Kojak! When it comes to Christmas presents, most people grow up to learn that not only is it more blessed to give then to receive — it's also more fun.

I saw this last Sunday when I spent the afternoon at the mall. Even though it was crowded and hectic, I saw that most people really had fun talking about what to buy: "Do you think so-and-so would like this?" "I don't know; she told me once that blue was her favorite color . . ." Most people enjoyed stopping to talk about someone else, and to decide what would be best to give her.

It's the giving that really makes Christmas fun. I read about it yesterday in the newspaper. A woman was in line at the supermarket when she saw a very poor, raggedy man up ahead of

her. He looked like he was homeless and he smelled like he hadn't been near a shower in a month. He was reaching into his pocket for some dimes and nickels so he could buy a loaf of day-old bread and a jar of sale-priced peanut butter. Quickly, she went up to him and gave him twenty dollars worth of food. His eyes lit up like he had just won the state lottery! He was filled with gratitude he could not express. And the woman felt good herself. She said it was the high point of her Christmas — the feeling she got from giving. She noted that many people who get so much each year seem to appreciate it so little.

Giving really is much more fun, so . . . What are you giving this year? Think back to the things you've bought, things that are hidden in your closets or lying under your tree. What are you giving for Christmas this year? What presents are you most anxious to see opened tomorrow, just so you can see the expression on a loved one's face?

Well, if we have this much fun giving material gifts to one another, how much more fun would we have giving spiritual gifts? Considering all the time and money we spend giving worldly gifts that wither and fade, how much more rewarding would it be to give spiritual gifts which last forever because they come from God?

Who will give the gift of forgiveness this year? Everybody needs it — no family, no marriage, no friendship of any kind can do without it. When it's so easy to hurt the ones we love, and sometimes so hard to forgive the ones we love the most, who will be the peacemaker when one is needed? Who will give the gift that heals old wounds and stops new wounds from bleeding?

Jesus Christ is born tonight to give us our forgiveness, that we may give it to one another. He tells us to forgive the people who wrong us "seven times seventy times." He teaches us to pray saying, *"Forgive us our trespasses, as we forgive those who trespass against us."* And finally, He even says it from the Cross: *"Father forgive them, for they know not what they do."*

I hope someone has forgiveness on their Christmas list this year. I've seen a lot of homes with too many fine dishes and fancy furs. I've never seen a home with too much forgiveness.

Who will give the gift of encouragement this year? Everybody needs it. We all need to know that someone else is pulling for us and wishing us the best. We all need some help along the way. When it's so easy to take the people we love for granted, who will offer a word of praise for a job well done or a word of thanks for a thoughtful gesture? Who will give the gift of being a positive and uplifting influence on someone else's life?

Jesus Christ is born tonight to give us our encouragement, that we may give it to one another. He is born to say, as He said so long ago, *"Rise up and walk. Open your eyes and see. Come unto Me all who are weary and heavy laden, and I will give you rest."*

I hope someone has encouragement on their Christmas list this year. I've seen a lot of homes with too many toys and too many gadgets for grown-up girls and boys. I've never seen a home with too much encouragement.

And who will offer the gift of love this year? Everybody needs love, and I'm not talking about physical love or lust tonight. I'm not talking about the romantic "good feeling" love they sing about on the radio. I'm talking about deep, abiding Christian love. When it's so easy just to think about yourself in this world, who will give the gift of love this year?

Jesus Christ is born tonight to give us God's love, that we may give it to one another. He said, *"As the Father has loved Me, so have I loved you; continue in My love."* Who will say to a parent or child or husband or wife, "You can count on me today and always, for better or for worse, in sickness and in health; I'll be here for you as Christ is here for me . . . because I love you?"

I hope someone has love on their Christmas list this year. I've seen a lot of homes with too many material things of every description. I've never seen a home with too much love.

Spiritual gifts like forgiveness and encouragement and love are given to us on this silent, holy night. They cannot be found in any store. They can't be purchased at any price. They can only be given to others, as Christ gives them to each of us.

Take a look at the people you are sitting with tonight. Think about other friends and loved ones who are close to your heart. There are worldly gifts and spiritual gifts. What are you giving for Christmas this year? Amen

# Some Assembly Required

**Old Testament Text:** Malachi 3:1-5
**New Testament Text:** Luke 2:25-35

*But who can endure the day of His coming, and who can stand when He appears? (Malachi 3:2)*

Some of you might know from your own experience that there are three words which can give a parent serious nightmares. Three words can drive real fear into a parent's heart. I'm talking about mothers and fathers cringing in abject terror at the mere sound of three simple words: "Some Assembly Required."

How well I learned this on Christmas Eve when I engaged in fierce hand-to-hand combat with a hobby horse! It came in a large box and was meant to be our children's big present this year. They can climb into the saddle and bounce up and down, pretending to chase imaginary outlaws. Every child should have a hobby horse, and we hoped our kids would be happy with theirs.

Well, about ten o'clock that night, after we were home from church and the little ones were asleep, I pulled this huge hobby horse box out from its hiding place. I put on some nice music and eagerly settled down to enjoy performing a parent's ritual on Christmas Eve.

Then I looked at the box, and right away, I knew I was in deep, deep, trouble. There in big, bold letters, were those three fatal words: "Some Assembly Required."

The horse and the eight-piece metal stand looked simple enough. But at the bottom of the box were three large plastic bags full of screws and plastic washers and safety hooks, and I don't know what else. The hobby horse company had thoughtfully provided me with 4,176 parts to put together. Because my training is in the ministry and not mechanical engineering, I knew I was in for a very long evening . . . "Some Assembly Required." Ha!

Think about what you do when you put a toy together. First, you spread the 4,176 pieces across the floor to see what you have to work with. Then, you look for the directions. You have to follow directions. You have to understand what the creator intended for the toy if you are to put the thing together as it was designed.

But we live in an imperfect world — a world still tainted by the fall into original sin. This means that nothing is perfect, so some of the 4,176 pieces you need must be missing. Evidently, this is part of the ritual of assemblying toys. It's a test of your temper and your resourcefulness when you find you have too many of one part and not enough of another.

Four hours later — at two o'clock in the morning — the job is done. The 4,176 pieces which once lay scattered across the floor are joined with pieces scrounged from your tool box, and everything is in its place. You have learned that "Some Assembly Required" is the grossest understatement of the Christmas season; but when the battle with the hobby horse is over, you stand back and admire your handiwork. Now you are ready for Christmas.

Christmas is said to be over when all the hobby horses and plastic battle cruisers and dresses and ties are opened. And what a letdown it can be when it's over! The tree comes down and the bright lights are put away. There are no more Advent candles in church, no more Christmas music in the air. And the hobby horse carefully put together with 4,176 pieces sits neglected because the toys that really capture your children's interests are the small plastic cartoon figures which cost $5.95 each.

But during the week after Christmas, the Christmas story has only just begun! Jesus Christ is born! The long-awaited

Messiah has come, and now that He is here, what difference will He make in our lives? How is everything different than it was before?

Some churches are content to sell the good feelings of the Christmas story and the infant Jesus, while ignoring the demands a grown-up Jesus places on our lives. This is a tragic temptation which shows how shallow and superficial religion can become. For those churches and those Christians, the Christmas story is over just as the Christmas shopping season is over, and it's back to business as usual.

But in our text from Luke, we see how the story of Jesus continues. We see that even Mary is not given very long to bask in the afterglow of that glorious and mysterious night. Now Joseph and Mary are in Jerusalem, to present their first-born in the temple and to offer a sacrifice according to the Law. And while they are there, they have a disturbing encounter with a stranger named Simeon, who makes them look into the future.

The little we know about Simeon comes from this story. He is a very old man by the time we meet him. He is "righteous and devout." Most significantly, Simeon has adopted a singularly important goal in life: he is "looking for the consolation of Israel." He's been told by the Holy Spirit that he won't die before he sees the Messiah, the Lord's Christ. That's what Simeon is living for. While most people are thinking only of getting ahead or "getting theirs," Simeon is looking for God.

Mary and Joseph must have felt their hearts swell with pride to see this old man search them out in this way. All the discomfort of the Bethlehem stable must have faded and their spirits must have soared when Simeon held the baby and praised His name:

> Lord, now lettest Thou Thy servant depart in peace,
>     according to Thy Word;
> For mine eyes have seen Thy salvation which Thou
> hast prepared in the presence of all peoples . . . (Luke 2:29-31)

But then Simeon goes on to show the darker, deeper side to the meaning of Christmas. Filled with the Holy Spirit, he says:

> *Behold, this child is set for the fall and rising*
> *of many in Israel, and for a sign that is spoken against . . .*
> *that thoughts out of many hearts may be revealed. (Luke*
> *2:34-35)*

Finally, Simeon looks deep into Mary's eyes and says, *"A sword will pierce your side also." (Luke 2:35)*

Who "also" will be pierced? Simeon is saying that a sword will pierce Jesus' side! His words point beyond the romantic manger scene to the Cross. He looks beyond Bethlehem to Calvary.

A lot of people walking the streets of Jerusalem that day must have stopped to admire the baby Jesus, to stroke His chin and call Him cute. Babies are so warm and appealing, so unassuming and vulnerable. They can't challenge us; they only depend on us and respond to our love. It's easy to love a baby, and it's easy to worship Jesus Christ as a newborn child.

But how many people, like Simeon, would also love the man Jesus grew up to be, i.e., the full-grown Jesus — not just as Friend and Savior, but as Prophet and Judge? *"Who can endure the day of His coming, and who can stand when He appears?"*

We cannot celebrate the coming of this child without also celebrating why He came and what He did when He got here. He came to "scatter the proud" and "exalt the lowly." He came to carry a Cross, to offer us the gift and the challenge of salvation.

Jesus came to change us, and to change the world — to call us away from the ways of death to the ways of life. He came to make us new — to re-assemble us as our Creator intends us to be. And which one of us doesn't need to be re-assembled today? Who among us is already completely put together in all of our parts, as the fully-constructed Christians God intends us to be?

Well, some Christians feel they are completely assembled. They call themselves "saved" and "sanctified" and removed from the stain of sin, as if God has already made them into everything He wants them to be. Whatever God did to change them has already been done, and now they are "blessed" and "saved."

But Jesus blesses those who *don't* feel that way. Jesus says, *"Blessed are the poor in spirit"* — blessed are those who feel incomplete and unworthy in the sight of God, for these are the ones He comes to seek! So, how about you? Where does your life need to be changed and re-arranged by God, now that He is here?

Is your faith and your coming to church a living, growing experience — or is it merely a habit, a matter of custom and convention? Do you live your faith at home and at work — or do you separate your Sunday morning faith from what you do during the rest of the week?

Are you doing your best to make Christ real to the people around you — or is there nothing about the example you set which would tell people you believe in Him? Do you keep an active prayer life — or do you take God's Word for granted?

Do you have the moral imagination to love your neighbor as yourself — even the neighbor who is far off and unfamiliar — or can you only be moved to compassion by people near and dear to you? Do you have a faith which asks what you can do for God, or do you only care about what God can do for you?

The truth is that we *"all have sinned and fall short of the glory of God." (Romans 3:23)* In one way or another, each of us is like that hobby horse with the 4,176 pieces. We each come wrapped in boxes plainly labeled: "Some Assembly Required." We all come with some spiritual pieces missing, and we can only be re-assembled by following the directions written by our Creator. This is how we are, and we only diminish the majesty and holiness of God by claiming more for ourselves than that.

Our other Scripture reading has much the same message this morning. The prophet Malachi says that God will be doing the assembly work still required, now that He is here. God is *"like a refiner's fire and the fuller's soap; He will sit as a refiner and purifier of silver, and He will purify the sons of Levi and refine them like gold and silver till they present right offerings to the Lord."* (Malachi 3:2-3)

Most importantly, Malachi does not diminish God's holiness by claiming his own virtue. Instead, he speaks before the Lord in honesty and humility: *"Who can endure the day of His coming, and who can stand when He appears?"* (Malachi 3:2)

When people tell me that they are "saved," I say to them: "Well, I'm glad for you, but I'm still a sinner. I'm still struggling to be purified and refined in God's sight. God is patient with me, and He lets me come before Him *just as I am, without one plea.* But as I look at myself in the light of God's glory, I know I still can't make a right offering to the Lord."

Who can really say that they are finished with the Christmas story of salvation? Who can say that God has come to earth because He is satisfied with who they are? Who says they can *"endure the day of His coming, and . . . stand when He appears?"*

To my way of thinking, the Christmas season is over, but the Christmas story has only just begun. Now God is with us, and what will we do? I don't know about you, but the package I come in still has written on it, in plain letters: "Some Assembly Required." I don't know about you, but I agree with the words Joel Hemphill wrote in his gospel song, "He's Still Working On Me":

> *There really ought to be a sign upon my heart,*
> *"Don't judge him yet, there's an unfinished part."*
> *But I'll be perfect according to His plan,*
> *Refashioned by my Master's loving hand.*

Amen

# Pastoral Prayer

Gracious God, we thank You for the spiritual blessings we have received this Christmas season. We prepared for Your coming and felt the mystery of the moment. We sang Your praises and warded off the darkness with Your light. Keep our minds and our hearts fixed on what You have done in that Bethlehem stable, that we may follow in our Lord's example as He grows in wisdom and stature.

Almighty God, who hears every cry and answers every need, we also pray today for those who are not happy or fulfilled this holiday season:

. . . for those who are separated from loved ones, and for those who felt the pangs of loneliness amid the holiday cheer.

. . . for all who were sick this past Christmas, and for those who were hungry or cold . . . for those who were too poor to buy presents, and those who were reminded in this holiday season of how little they have while others have so much.

Finally, dear Lord, we pray for ourselves, one and all, who come before You spiritually incomplete, with some assembly still required. Keep us from any form of spiritual pride which might leave us satisfied with who we are. Make us poor in spirit and humble of faith, that we may know the Kingdom of Heaven. Fill us with the desire to be built up and refashioned by Your hand, that we may be used mightily in the work of Your kingdom here on earth. In Jesus' name. Amen

# The Girl Who Was Too Smart to Learn

*Now there was a man in Jerusalem whose name was Simeon . . .*
*[who was] looking for the consolation of Israel . . . (Luke 2:25)*

Once upon a time, there was a young girl who was very, very smart. Even when she was a baby, people knew she was unusually bright, since she was walking and talking much sooner than other babies. Everyone could see that this girl was special.

When she was only three, her mother began teaching her to read, and the little girl learned quickly. She read the easy books, like Doctor Seuss, and soon she was ready for something more difficult. But when her mother brought her some harder books to try, she said, "Mommy, I already know how to read; let me do something else."

She started taking piano lessons, and before long she was good enough to perform in a recital. Everyone marvelled at how well she played for such a young age, and they said that if she kept working at it, she would become a fine pianist some day. But the little girl wanted to stop taking lessons. "I already know how to play the piano," she said, "I want to do something else now."

Her father began teaching her how to play tennis. He took her out on the court every chance he got and she got better quickly. She won a tournament for children aged twelve and under, and everyone thought she had a great future in the sport. Her father wanted her to keep playing in order to reach the next level of ability, but the girl said, "No, Daddy, I already know how to play tennis. Let me do something else."

The little girl was too smart to learn . . . or, I should say, she *thought* she was too smart to learn. As soon as she knew a little bit about something, she figured she "knew it all" and had nothing else to learn. She didn't want to keep growing. She was content to stay where she was.

By contrast, the Bible tells us about someone named Simeon who never stopped learning and growing. Simeon was an old man when Jesus was born; but he wasn't too old to see something new in life. He wasn't too old to be led by faith in search of something more. Simeon had heard about the birth of God's Son, and even though he was already an old man, Simeon kept searching and seeking until he saw the baby Jesus with his own eyes.

We in the church hope you will always be like Simeon, and not like the girl who thought she was too smart to learn. Don't ever let yourself stop learning and growing in life! Don't stop listening to others or respecting what they tell you because you think you "know it all" . . . at home, in school, and especially in church.

I say "especially in church" because with faith more than anything else, it's important to keep learning and growing. You can never "know it all" about God. You can never know Jesus so well that you don't need to know Him better. When you are young as well as old, be like Simeon and keep searching for Jesus, in your heart and in the world. It will be the most exciting thing you do in life, and one day, as surely as Simeon, you will find yourself so close to your Lord as to see Him face to face. Amen

# About the Author

Erskine White is Senior Minister of the First Congregational Church in Melrose, Massachusetts. Known as a lively and dynamic preacher, he believes that good preaching rooted in Scripture is an integral part of church growth and spiritual vitality.

Prior to his present pastorate, Rev. White served inner city, urban and suburban congregations in Milwaukee, Wisconsin; Hartford, Connecticut; and Brookfield, Connecticut respectively. He worked as a community organizer for an ecumenical agency in African-American and Hispanic neighborhoods. Rev. White is also the first Protestant minister ever to serve on the national staff of the U.S. Catholic Church, having worked for four years in Washington, D.C. with the Campaign for Urban Development, United States Catholic Conference, the largest church anti-poverty program in the nation.

Rev. White graduated *cum laude* with High Honors from Middlebury College, Middlebury, Vermont in 1973. He received his M.Div. degree from the Yale University Divinity School four years later and was ordained to the ministry in the United Church of Christ. He has previously published more than a dozen articles in the religious and secular press.

He is married to Caroline Blackwell White; together, they are the parents of three young children: two boys, Daniel and Joshua, and one girl, Jordan.